Be proactive

(Step 1)

Plan your work

(Step 2)

Ten Steps
to Help You Write

BETTER ESSAYS & TERM PAPERS

Third Edition

NEIL SAWERS

Viva Books

New Delhi | Mumbai | Chennai | Kolkata | Bangalore | Hyderabad | Kochi

First Indian Edition 2009

VIVA BOOKS PRIVATE LIMITED

- 4737/23 Ansari Road, Daryaganj, New Delhi 110 002
  E-mail: vivadelhi@vivagroupindia.net, Tel. 42242200
- 76, Service Industries, Shirvane, Sector 1, Nerul, Navi Mumbai 400 706
  E-mail: vivamumbai@vivagroupindia.net, Tel. 27721273, 27721274
- Jamals Fazal Chambers, 26 Greams Road, Chennai 600 006
  E mail: vivachennai@vivagroupindia.net, Tel. 28290304, 28294241
- B-103, Jindal Towers, 21/1A/3 Darga Road, Kolkata 700 017
  E-mail: vivakolkata@vivagroupindia.net, Tel. 22836381, 22816713
- 7, Sovereign Park Apartments, 56-58, K. R. Road, Basavanagudi, Bangalore 560 004
  E-mail: vivabangalore@vivagroupindia.net, Tel. 26607409, 26607410
- 101-102 Mughal Marc Apartments, 3-4-637 to 641, Narayanguda, Hyderabad 500 029
  E-mail: vivahyderabad@vivagroupindia.net, Tel. 27564481, 27564482
- Beevi Towers, First Floor, SRM Road, Kaloor, Kochi 682 018, Kerala
  E-mail: vivakochi@vivagroupindia.net, Tel: 0484-2403055, 2403056

www.vivagroupindia.com

Published by arrangement with

The NS Group
21 - 10405 Jasper Avenue, Suite 586
Edmonton, AB
Canada
T5J 3S2

ISBN-10: 81-309-0511-6
ISBN-13: 978-81-309-0511-2

Published by Vinod Vasishtha for Viva Books Private Limited, 4737/23, Ansari Road, Daryaganj, New Delhi-110 002. Printed and bound by Anand Sons, Delhi-110 092.

Writing challenges many of us. We find it difficult to complete something, let alone get started, so fear can be a major factor. This booklet's purpose is to help you write more effectively and easily. Essays and term papers are the main focus. However, if you apply the tools and concepts in this booklet, it will make a difference with any writing you have, or wish, to do.

About this edition

In 2001, the American Psychological Association (APA) published the fifth edition of the APA Publication Manual. We have updated this booklet to reflect the changes in referencing from that edition.

We have also taken the opportunity to rework Step Four, "Identify Your Thesis," to provide better direction in this key area.

In terms of format, the right hand page provides detailed information. To help you remember this information, the left hand page highlights key points.

I'd like to acknowledge those who have guided me with this edition. In particular, Dr. Linda Leff, Coordinator of the OSU Writing Center, Oklahoma State University, Stillwater, Oklahoma, for her advice in the pre-writing section; Patrick O'Neill, President of Extraordinary Conversations Inc. of Toronto, for his advice in the listening and speaking section; Gillan Richards, Coordinator, Secondary Program, Algoma District School Board, Sault Ste. Marie, Ontario, for her advice in paragraph development; Catherine Scott, Ph.D. candidate, University of Waterloo English Department, for her advice in the thesis section; librarian, Laura Scott, for her advice in the research reference section. My final, special thank you, goes to Marilyn for continuing to support the vision of this booklet.

THE BASIC STEPS

There are two ***Basic Steps*** that can help you carry out your assignments more effectively. They are:

- **Be proactive**
- **Plan your work**

Be proactive deals with attitude and is all about boldness and initiative.

The second step, as its name indicates, is a ***planning*** step. What must you do, by when, to complete your work on time?

Proactivity:

Going out of your way
to seek out and take
the initiative

***Don't let fear stop
you from trying
something new***

STEP ONE

be proactive

The Concise Oxford Dictionary defines **proactive** as "creating or controlling a situation by taking the initiative."

Today's most successful people are always proactive whether in school, sports, music, business or any other field. For you, being proactive means going that extra step to complete your assignment successfully. For example:

- Doing that extra bit of research
- Calling up a newspaper editor or government expert to get a different slant on your topic when others wondered what you were doing
- Speaking to an instructor to clarify expectations for an assignment

Being proactive is about attitude. When you approach every assignment proactively, it usually becomes easier to complete and of higher quality.

Dealing with the negatives + the "fear" factor

The challenge many of us face are the negatives so often connected with essays and term papers. You believe it's going to be hard. Well-meaning instructors and textbooks reinforce this with comments like "You may find this a difficult assignment," "It's not easy," etc.

The answer? Go for the more positive "I can do this," and ignore what others think. So often, "fear" blocks us from moving forward; fear of change, fear of doing something different, it's too risky. I want to encourage you not to let fear stop you from trying something new.

I'm not so naïve as to suggest that things will always go smoothly. You will hit roadblocks. But if you say, "Yes, I can," your chances of producing the results you want are far better.

Each step in this booklet is designed to help you be proactive and get the job done.

One of the first ways to be ***proactive*** is...

Good planning
will help you

Plan based
on the due date
of your assignment

How many hours
will you need?

STEP TWO

plan your work

Here's the picture: you've got an essay due Monday and a paper at midterm. How do you make sure that you give yourself enough time to complete both by their due dates?

Some of us don't have a problem. We just figure it out and do it. Others leave things to the last minute. We know we have a deadline so we get very focused and the job gets done. This last minute stuff, however, can be stressful and you may not do your best work.

We live in a fast moving world where expectations from teachers and employers demand more results in less and less time. Essays and term papers, to do them justice, require focused effort. In my experience, it's easier to get the time if you plan for it in your schedule.

"What must I do, by when, to complete this assignment on time?"

Let's say you're given an assignment on November 4th to be turned in on the 12th. You have eight days to complete it. What steps should you take?

1. *Make your plan based on the date your assignment is due*

2. *Figure out how many hours it will take to carry out the assignment*

From your experience you have a rough idea how long it takes to do something. How much time for research and analysis? How much time for writing and revising? These figures may be only a "guesstimate", but at least they're a guide.

Due date ______________________________________

HOURS REQUIRED:	Min	Max	By When
Topic/Thesis	_____	_____	__________
Research	_____	_____	__________
Outline/Action plan	_____	_____	__________
Writing/Revision	_____	_____	__________
Contingency	_____	_____	__________
Total hours	_____	_____	__________

Work back from the due date to determine your start date

Prioritize your activities

When I estimate, I use "minimum" and "maximum" hours to give flexibility. I also add time for contingencies (emergencies) because other factors invariably come up to complicate things. For November 12th you might need:

	MINIMUM	MAXIMUM
Topic/Thesis	1.0	1.5
Research	2.5	3.0
Outline/Action plan	2.0	3.0
Writing/Revision	7.0	8.0
Contingency	1.0	2.0
TOTAL HOURS	**13.5**	**17.5**

3. *Determine your start date*

Let's say you need 15 hours to carry out the assignment. How many hours can you spare per day given other school and personal priorities? For our purposes, let's assume you have up to three hours per day. To get 15 hours, you will need five days to complete the assignment. At the latest, you'd have to begin your assignment by November 7th in order to hand it in on the 12th.

On the other hand, if you have time available, you could cram it all into a couple of days. At least you know your priorities and options.

Schedule the time in your calendar

Stick to the schedule or "work your plan"

4. *Schedule the time in your calendar*

However you decide to allocate your time, by slotting the hours into your calendar on a daily basis, you lock in the time required for your assignment. You may have to reshuffle other activities to fit within your priorities.

5. *Stick to the schedule or "work your plan"*

This requires self discipline. When you work your plan, however, you:

- Reduce pressure on yourself
- Avoid a time crunch
- Even out the work
- Build in flexibility
- Provide an opportunity for later review

Remember, time is precious, limited and yours. Use it well. The Clarifying Steps that follow will help you make the best use of your time.

Come up with the right topic

(Step 3)

Identify your thesis

(Step 4)

Do the research

(Step 5)

Develop the organization/outline

(Step 6)

THE CLARIFYING STEPS

There are four Clarifying Steps. They are:

- **Come up with the right topic**
- **Identify your thesis**
- **Do the research**
- **Develop the organization/outline**

The Clarifying Steps underpin the writing process. They're designed to help you get clear about:

a. The topic you're choosing

b. What you intend to prove about it, and,

c. How to carry it out.

The order of these steps is not locked in. You can just as easily be researching the topic, identifying your thesis, or organizing your ideas at the same time.

Why the "up front" clarifying work is so important

If you take the time to do the "up front" work before you start writing a draft, it invariably pays off.

Whenever I approach writing for myself or clients, I almost always use mind mapping and brainstorming. I then research the assignment to see what I can find out about it. I'll write a lot down, I'll talk to people, I'll read, I'll explore library reference sections and I'll check the Internet.

I was recently asked to do a short piece on Madonna to the effect that her impact on the music scene of the eighties and nineties would be short lived. After exploring the topic, I came to the conclusion that the thesis "Madonna - forgotten in the new Millennium," was not viable. The client agreed and the piece was written from an opposite view.

One way to explain the importance of doing this "up front" work, is through triangle diagrams, often used to demonstrate success in sales.

Normal triangle

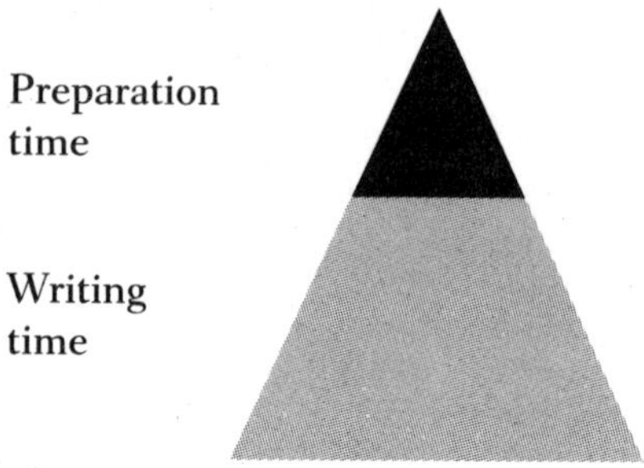

Scattered focus

Inverted triangle

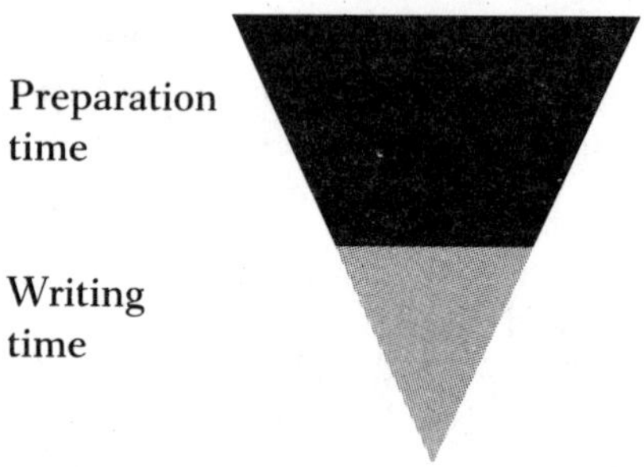

More focus

Normal triangle - lack of required information

Too often a salesperson tries to close a sale quickly without uncovering the wants and needs of the customer. For example, in the auto industry, some salespeople try and "fit" the car to the customer. Because they only spend a small amount of time (the apex of the triangle) in determining needs, it is much harder to close the sale. The customer is confused and has lots of questions and objections. The broad base of the triangle indicates this scattered focus and direction.

Inverted triangle - emphasizes up front work

In the inverted triangle, the salesperson takes the time to find out exactly what the customer needs and wants. What is the customer to use this vehicle for? City or highway driving? Kids to baseball practice or dance classes? What budget? Whatever the needs and wants the salesperson takes the time to uncover them. The salesperson then points out the vehicles that will fit those needs. The broad base of the inverted triangle emphasizes the value of that "up front" work and points down to the apex. The result is clear focus and direction. The sale is much easier to make.

The lesson of the inverted triangle

When you don't do the work "up front" - ***normal triangle*** - your focus is scattered. When you do the "up front" work - ***inverted triangle*** - your focus is on where you want to go.

This same "rule" applies to writing essays and term papers. If you spend more time to get clear from the start where you're going and how to get there, doing the necessary research/analysis and obtaining key information, you'll require less time and effort for the actual writing. You will be more focused.

Topic Criteria:

- In your study area
- Interests you
- Is of value
- Accepted by your instructor

STEP THREE

come up with the right topic

For some people, this step is rarely a problem. For others, coming up with the right topic is challenging and can create mental blocks. We hope to change that by providing a pathway to assist you.

Who selects the topic?

The topic is either:

1. Chosen after discussion between you and your instructor
2. Determined by your instructor
3. Selected by you alone

If your instructor has determined the topic, your job is to think about that topic, research it and come up with a thesis - i.e. what you want to prove about the topic.

If you're choosing the topic

When the choice of topic has been left completely or partly with you, how should you choose? Whenever possible, your topic should meet four basic criteria:

- *Be in your area of study*
- *Interest you* - i.e. you're excited about it - you enjoy it
- *Be of value* - i.e. you have something valuable to communicate
- *Accepted as suitable by your instructor*

Sometimes you know exactly the topic you want to cover. Other times you're not sure, don't know, or you're blocked. We've all been there. I suggest that you literally go on an exploration to uncover that topic, using some very practical techniques along with some remarkable tools.

Please do not let fear stop you from trying these tools & techniques

Explore to uncover the topic

Relax and give yourself time to think

PRACTICAL TECHNIQUES FOR EXPLORING A TOPIC

Before we begin, a reminder about fear. In Step One, "Be Proactive," on page 5, I stressed the importance of not letting "fear" stop you from doing things that make a difference. The techniques and tools that follow, if you use them, will make a difference in the quality of your efforts and your satisfaction at doing your best. Please do not be afraid to try them. They work.

Thinking

The first practical technique is your own thinking. By that I mean thinking while relaxed.

We're usually so busy that we don't believe there's enough time to sit back and think about what we're trying to accomplish. Many successful people, however, regularly take breaks from what they're doing simply to focus their attention on new subjects, or areas that they're concerned about.

I recommend that you give yourself some quiet time to reflect. Take a walk, sit back at home, go have coffee somewhere - and let your mind flow free. Ideas have a chance to surface, patterns start to emerge, relationships begin to form.

Always carry a notebook so that you can jot your ideas down and not forget them.

While you're thinking, consider your reader. What is it your reader is expecting? (We cover the reader more fully in *Step 7 - Write with your reader in mind.*)

Time to think like this is valuable at any stage; whether you're researching the topic, wondering what your thesis will be, or simply organizing and writing your presentation.

Explore with pre-writing

Explore through research

Exploration tools

- Brainstorming
- Mind mapping
- Rapidwriting

Pre-writing

Pre-writing is a second practical way to explore. Pre-writing simply means doing some exploratory writing in the topic area. Many teachers encourage this because, like thinking, it can open up your mind to other possibilities. Things you write down can jell into a topic that can seem promising (or not) and uncover ideas, insights and options that you may not have considered before.

How much time should you take for this "up front" work? That depends on how many hours, days or weeks you have for the whole assignment. I suggest you build in time to pre-write - even if it's only half an hour to an hour. Increase the time based on the size and scope of the assignment.

Research

A third practical way is through research. Research, which we'll cover more fully in Step 5, can also open up new ideas, send you off in a different direction, or confirm where you're headed. Is a topic worth pursuing? Is there enough material? Research may provide an answer.

TOOLS TO HELP YOU EXPLORE

The following tools will fully support your efforts, not just in school or college, but in whatever you do. They are:

- Brainstorming
- Mind mapping
- Rapidwriting

These three tools make use of the random and often remarkable ways in which our minds come up with different thoughts and ideas. They allow us to get these thoughts and ideas down on paper, and in the case of mind mapping, display them in an organized manner. By using these tools in your exploration process, you will most likely become clear:

a. About your topic,

b. What you want to prove about it, and

c. How to organize/outline it for writing.

Brainstorming rules:

- Write down every idea
- No censorship
- No judgment
- No evaluation
- No editing

Evaluate each idea
then pick the topic with
the best potential

Brainstorming

Brainstorming is a freewheeling session, by yourself or with others, in which you focus on a topic or area you wish to examine more closely. In this session you let every idea about the topic come up, and, no matter how far fetched or crazy it seems, you write it down.

Start with a clear desk and a clean sheet of paper. If you prefer a chalkboard, flip chart or computer, use that instead.

If two or three of you are working together, it helps if one person acts as a recorder, making sure that everything the group thinks of is written down.

Do's and don'ts while brainstorming

- Do write down each idea, one after the other
- Don't censor yourself
- Don't evaluate or judge anything
- Don't edit anything
- If friends or classmates assist you, don't let them censor, judge or edit either

Review the results

Once the ideas are down:

- Evaluate what you've got
- Eliminate those ideas that don't work
- Select the topic with the most potential from those that remain

Brainstorming is a great way to begin exploring options, especially when ideas are given unrestricted flow. Combining this technique with mind mapping, however, can really make a difference to your results.

Mind mapping:

- Write down main topic area in middle of page
- Create a branch for each different thought or idea
- Add ideas that pertain to existing branches to those branches
- If it's a totally new idea, create a new branch

Mind mapping

Mind mapping is one of the most valuable tools I have ever come across, not just for writing, but for planning and exploration of all kinds.

With mind mapping:

- The topic area you're exploring is written down in the middle of a sheet of paper or chalkboard.
- Every thought, every idea about that topic, or area of interest from which a topic might come, goes down on the paper or chalkboard as branches on a map. (The key points that come out of your notes, your research, what you've read - all get added to the branches.) It is these branches that give order and flow to your random thoughts and ideas.
- Each branch represents similar thoughts and ideas. Any new thought or idea pertaining to an existing branch is added to that branch.
- A totally new idea, with no relation to an existing branch, receives a branch of its own.

The result is like looking at a tree from above - you see a trunk with all kinds of branches spreading from it, each with its own categories of information.

Once your thoughts, ideas, notes, etc., are down on paper, you can analyze what you've got. Which are the most important branches? What connections are there between branches? Is there a logical place from which a topic could come?

See over the next few pages how these mind maps are created and evolve.

Initial mind map

- Subject in middle (healthier world)
- Branches (history, food & water, education, disease prevention)

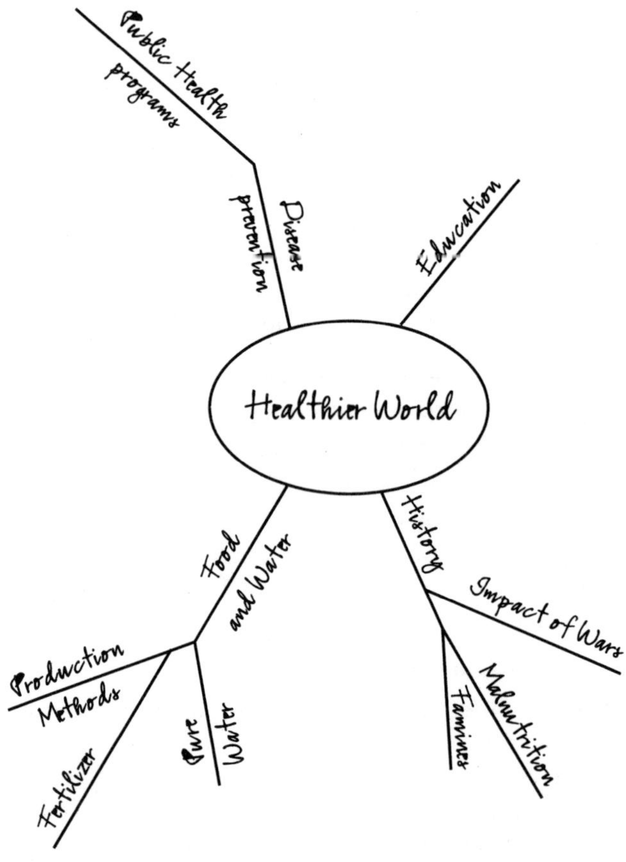

Mind Maps® is a Registered Trademark of the Buzan Centres - used here with enthusiastic permission.

APPLICATION

I'm going to give you two practical examples. The first uses the mind map approach we've just covered. The second uses a unique way of using Post-it® Notes created by 3M company. It's called "Using sticky notes."

Mind map approach

Let's assume that as part of a sociology program you have to write something about the improved health of the world compared to the turn of the last century. The topic is in that area but you're unsure what it will be. Here's how to begin using the mind map process:

Take a clean sheet of paper, or chalkboard and in the middle, write down the area you want to explore. In this case write "healthier world."

Immediately your mind starts to conjure up thoughts about health in its many permutations. Because it's such a large subject you decide to focus on health in the developing world.

What health problems did countries in the developing world face? That historical perspective is your first branch - and some of the sub topics that you might come up with include malnutrition, tropical diseases, childhood diseases, dysentery, etc.

With your pen or chalk, you place this first branch off the central core. Now you brainstorm other areas which may require new branches, or additions to branches you've already created.

- There's a *disease prevention* branch - every thought or idea about how diseases were prevented over the last 100 years goes down here; vaccines, better professional care, purifying the water, controlling sewage. These measures helped lessen death and disease, creating a healthier population with more children surviving and older people living longer.

Mind Map (Complete)

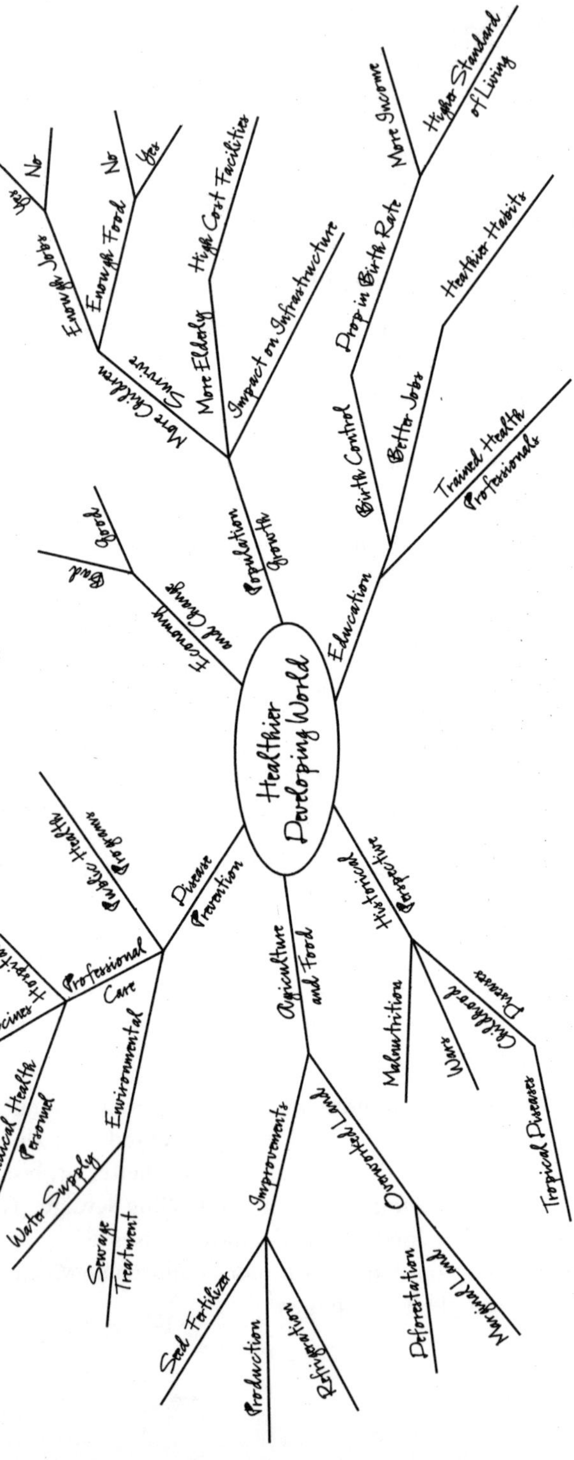

- You recognize that *education* played a major role - so that's a new branch. Included in that branch are public health programs, the training of medical professionals and other health workers, environmental health, etc.
- There's an *agriculture & food* branch. The century has seen dramatic improvements in agriculture and food production. There's better seed, fertilizers and production methods creating more food. On the other hand there's land that's unable to support a growing population because of poor quality soils, flooding, lack of water, erosion from deforestation, etc.
- There's a *population* branch. There are more children because of vaccines, better hygiene and better food & water. On the other hand, lower death rates have increased the population. In some countries the food supply can't keep up, leading to malnutrition, starvation and death.
- There's an *economy* branch. How has the increased population affected the economy? Are there more jobs? Are jobs scarce? Has it been a drain on national resources?

As you let your mind wander, you'll find that your ideas come from all kinds of different places. Add those ideas to the branches you've created. If it's a totally new idea, remember to create another branch.

Using sticky notes

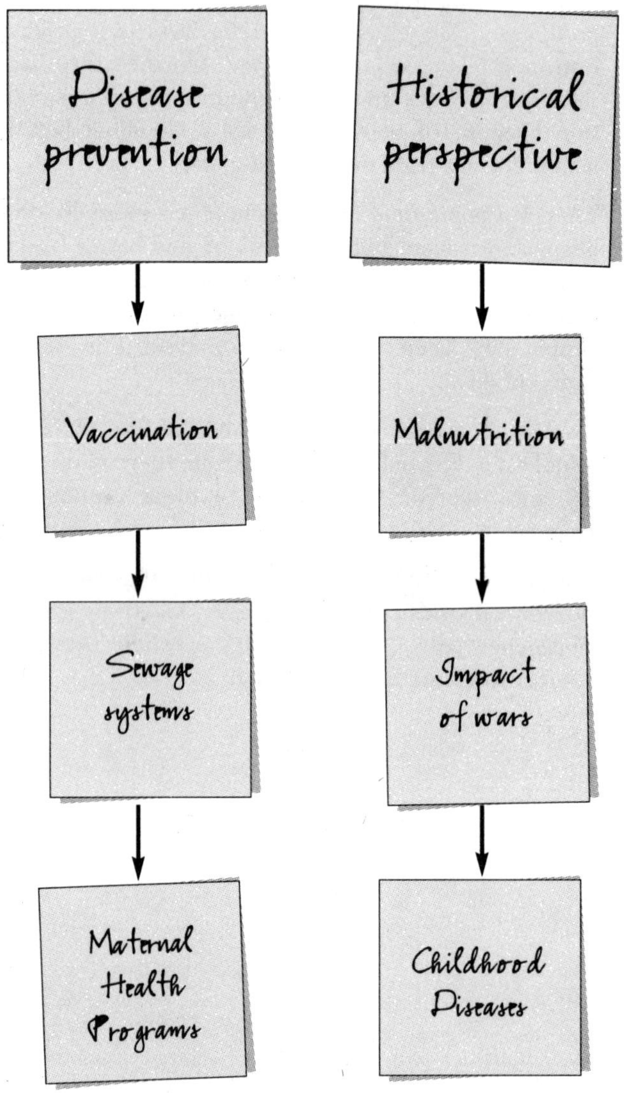

Using sticky notes

From the previous example we write down each key point on a sticky note. We then put it on a surface like a flip chart or wall. Flip charts work well because the size of the paper gives plenty of space.

Now, instead of branches you create rows or columns, each row or column representing a branch. Personally, I find columns easier to use.

- At the top of the column, place a general heading of what that column is about
- Every sticky note pertaining to that column goes underneath it
- Create a new column if it's a different area altogether
- Use as many columns as there are branches

On the following double page, you can see what happens with all the information when using sticky notes.

Using Sticky Notes (Complete)

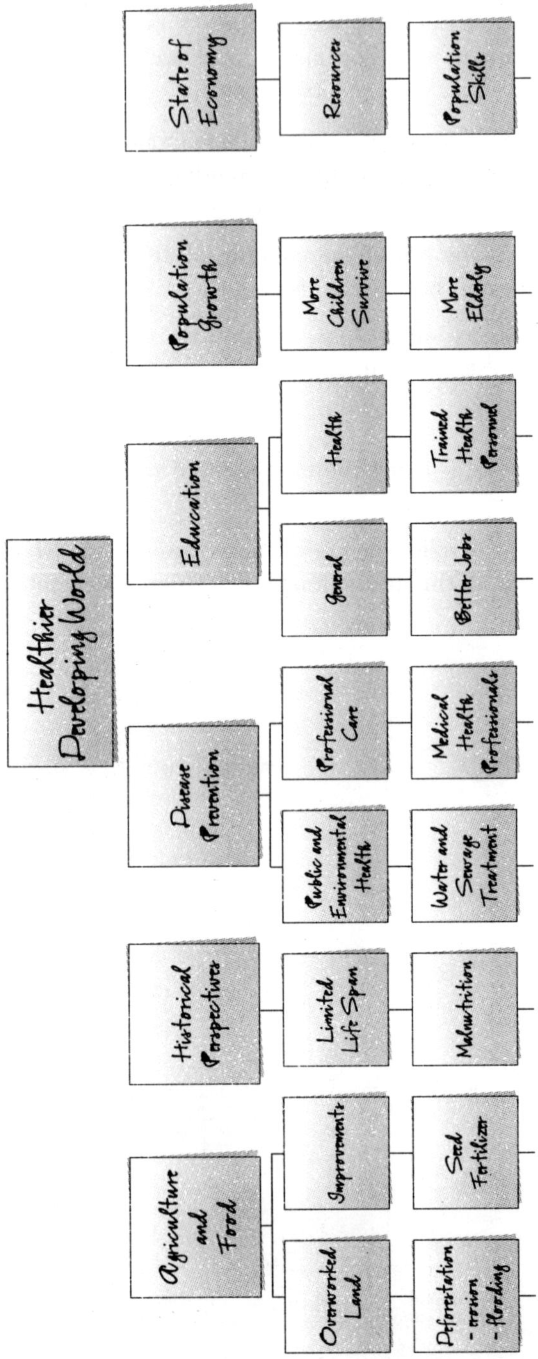

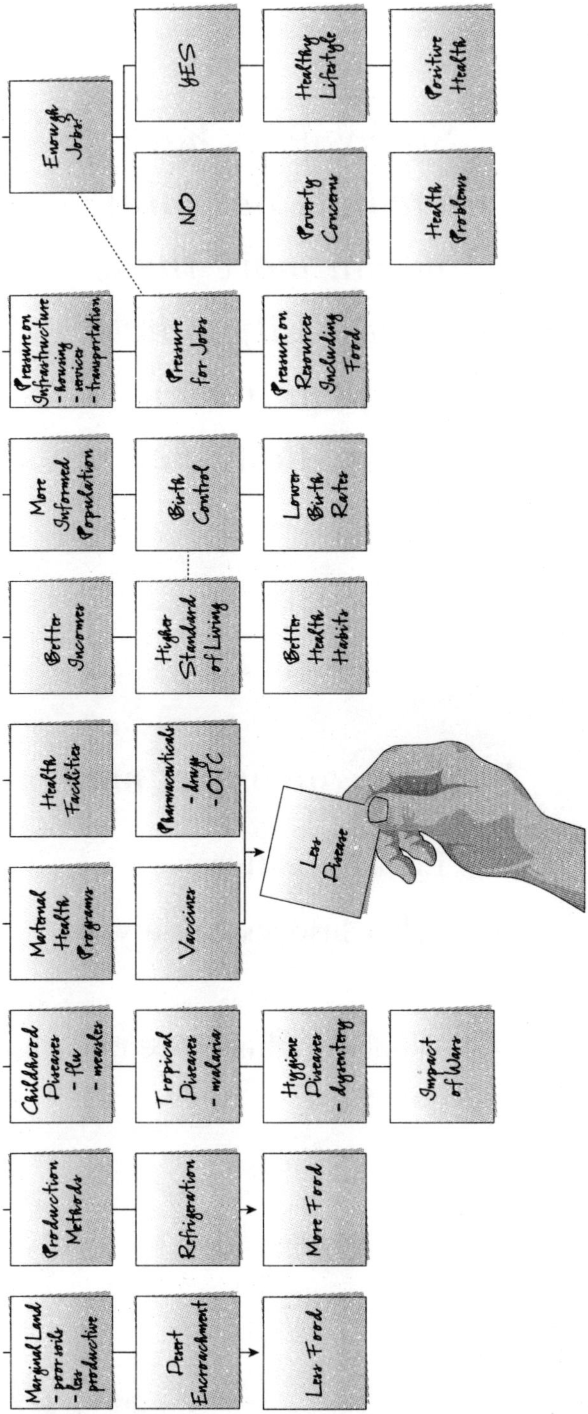
Marginal Land
- poor soils
- less productive
Desert Encroachment
Less Food
Production Methods
Refrigeration
More Food
Childhood Diseases
- flu
- measles
Tropical Diseases
- malaria
Hygiene Diseases
- dysentery
Impact of Wars
Maternal Health Programs
Vaccines
Health Facilities
Pharmaceuticals
- drugs
- OTC
Less Disease
Better Incomes
Higher Standard of Living
Better Health Habits
More Informed Population
Birth Control
Lower Birth Rates
Pressure on Infrastructure
- housing
- services
- transportation
Pressure for Jobs
Pressure on Resources Including Food
Enough Jobs?
NO
Poverty Concerns
Health Problems
YES
Healthy Lifestyle
Positive Health

Sticky notes have incredible flexibility. You can move them around easily to help you plan, review, create flow, etc.

Analyze your mind map:

- Look for patterns
- What bridges could you create?
- What conclusions could you draw?

Now here's the magic of using sticky notes. Because of the unique quality of the product, you can:

- Move a sticky note around
- If something doesn't fit in one column and belongs in another, you can move it there
- Move items around in an individual column until you're satisfied that the items are in a sequence that you can work with

Conventional mind map system or use sticky notes?

For me, the connections are more visible on the conventional system, especially when I'm dealing with only a few branches. If you have a lot of branches, however, with many sub headings, sticky notes may be more manageable.

Mind map analysis

Once the information is down, analyze what you've got. Look for patterns. How does one branch (or column if you use sticky notes) relate to another? What bridges could you create? What other connections are there? What conclusions could you draw?

In my experience, when you create a mind map, the important things seem to jump out at you. You start to see how and where all your thoughts, ideas and research connect together. A direction for the topic and what you want to prove about it, shows up.

This helps you determine the sequence of your essay or term paper and often gives you ideas and connections, even conclusions, that you might not have considered.

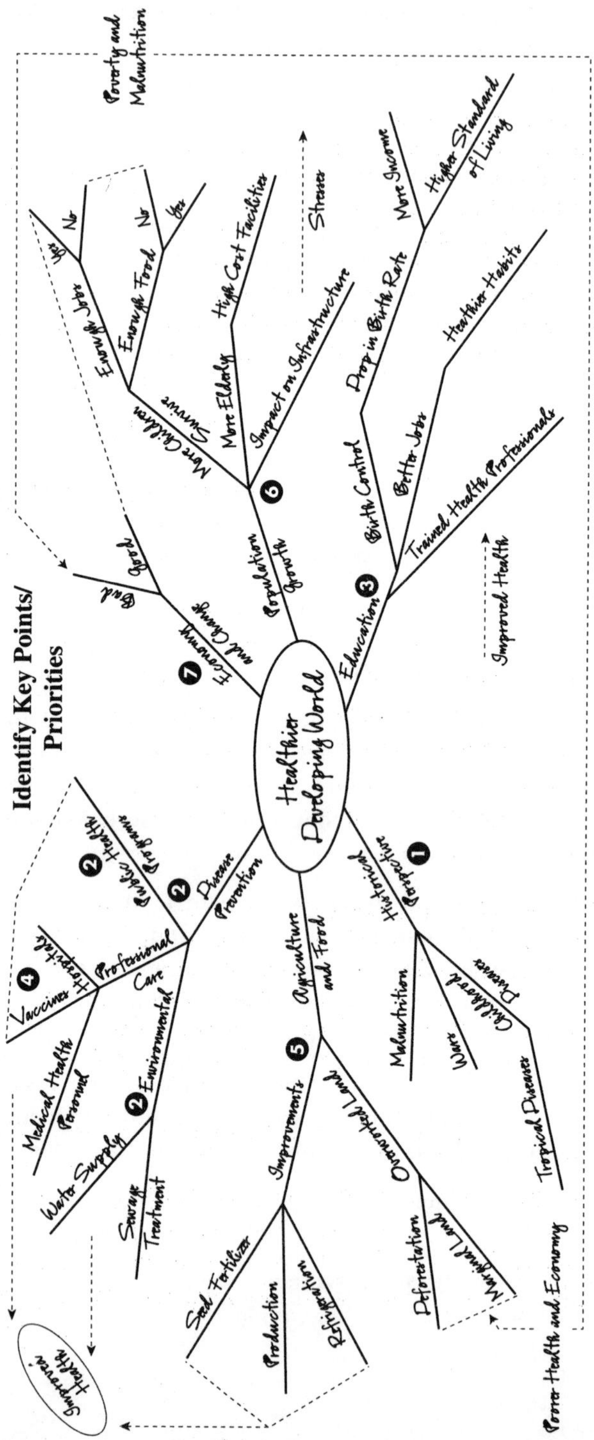
Identify Key Points/
Priorities
Healthier Developing World
1 Historical Perspective
Malnutrition
Wars
Childhood Diseases
Tropical Diseases
Poorer Health and Economy
2 Disease Prevention
2 Public Health Programme
Professional Care
Hospitals
4 Vaccines
Medical Health Personnel
2 Environmental
Water Supply
Sewage Treatment
Improved Health
5 Agriculture and Food
Improvements
Seed Fertilizer
Production
Refrigeration
Overworked Land
Deforestation
Marginal Land
3 Education
Birth Control
Drop in Birth Rate
More Income
Higher Standard of Living
Better Jobs
Heathier Habits
Trained Health Professionals
Improved Health
6 Population Growth
More Children Survive
Enough Jobs
Yes
No
Enough Food
No
Yes
More Elderly
High Cost Facilities
Impact on Infrastructure
Stresses
Poverty and Malnutrition
7 Economy and Change
Good
Bad

You may also see where too much emphasis has been applied in one area and too little in another. If one area looks thin, you might need more research, or, question whether to go down a particular path.

Identify key points and/or priorities

Next, identify the key points, or priorities. In which sequence should they be discussed? By numbering them you give yourself the natural, step by step, linear sequence that you can work with when writing your first draft.

Here's how that might work using the health care example. If you look at the mind map on the opposite page, you will see that I have numbered certain areas because to me they are the key points or priorities with which to deal. I see "historical perspectives" as the first priority, followed by "disease prevention" - notably basic areas like public health programs and environmental concerns such as water supply and treatment of sewage.

If we assume that our topic is "The impact of health care in the developing world over the last 100 years," here are the key points in sequence, as identified on the mind map:

1. Historical health problems
2. Importance of disease prevention in improving health, specifically public health & environmental programs
3. Public education - in both health and general terms and its benefits
4. Health care resources - people and resources
5. Improved agriculture/food production
6. Impact of population growth - stress on infrastructure, land, transportation, etc.
7. Impact of changes on the economy

It is this seven key point sequence that you can now use in developing or organizing your material so as to write your first draft.

Try **rapidwriting** *to uncover fresh thoughts and ideas about your topic... it only takes a few minutes*

Rapidwriting rules:

- Write nonstop
- No censoring
- No correcting
- No judgment

Review what you wrote:

- Highlight key points to add to your mind map/ organizing

Rapidwriting

I'd like to introduce you to one more tool. It's called rapidwriting (or freewriting) and it can be very useful in giving you fresh ideas about your topic.

Although similar to brainstorming, with rapidwriting you let the mind flow with the topic, doing anything it wants, writing down insights, making comparisons - all without limitation. Nothing is taboo. You can make judgments and evaluations; you can express your views in the moment.

In rapidwriting you write, nonstop, for a fixed period of time. Here are the rules:

- Give yourself a time frame - it might be five minutes, 15 minutes, half an hour - to write about your topic. (Some believe you can only focus for a few minutes. I find that I can go 15 minutes or more when I hit my stride. Whatever works for you is fine.)
- Don't stop - just let the words and ideas flow
- Don't censor yourself
- Don't decide if what you've written is good or bad
- Don't change anything, don't correct, don't say, "I shouldn't have written that!"

When the time is up, examine what you've written. I am amazed at the wealth of information that can be generated from this simple exercise. Underline or highlight the key points and add this new information to your mind map, or however you organize your work.

Summary

These techniques - brainstorming, mind mapping, rapidwriting - can be used at any time for many different purposes. They are extremely valuable in helping you get clear about where you're going.

Is your topic viable?

- Check it
- Test it
- Will it fly?
- Are there holes big enough to drive a truck through?

IS THE TOPIC VIABLE?

Before you finalize your topic, make sure it's viable. In business they test something by making a prototype or giving a new service a trial run prior to committing full resources to a project. An example from the aircraft industry is the "chicken test." When aircraft take off or land, birds are sometimes sucked into the intakes of jet engines. Manufacturers have to be certain that an engine will keep running if birds are a problem. So, they fire dead chickens into the intake of an engine prototype. If the engine continues to perform satisfactorily, the project continues.

Another wonderful phrase I heard for reviewing a film script could also apply: "Are there holes big enough in your topic to drive a truck through?"

What test will you apply to your topic to see if it's viable?

Is what I'm working on good enough to fly? Can I drive a truck through it? Do I have enough research to back up my opinions or to challenge them? Can I develop this topic in enough depth or am I wasting my time? By discovering any shortcomings early, you save yourself time. Then, you can start looking for a fresh angle to your topic, or a new topic entirely.

Consider limiting (or expanding) your topic so as to focus better on a specific area

How might you narrow down and define your topic effectively?

LIMITING (OR EXPANDING) THE TOPIC

You could write a book on some topics. On the other hand, you may find that you have to expand the topic for your discussion to be of value.

I'm going to concentrate on the need to limit a topic - a topic that might otherwise cover too much ground. By determining limits, you narrow the focus. This lets you fully explore and develop a specific area.

For example, when we discussed mind mapping we suggested a topic for sociology about the improved health of the world today compared to 1900. Since it was such a broad topic, we narrowed it down to "health in the developing world."

Even that's a very broad topic. We could narrow it down even more by considering only the health of "children" in the developing world.

We could further limit the topic by discussing "the impact of vaccination programs" on these children.

You can also narrow down a specific assignment given by your instructor. Suppose your English essay was "Hamlet: insane or just faking it?" The focused version might be "What does Hamlet's relationship with Ophelia tell us of the central character and his state of mind?"

In summary, the reason for narrowing or limiting a topic is because the scope is usually too broad to allow more detailed analysis and discussion.

If a topic won't fit,
don't try to force it

Do you know what
your instructor expects
from you?

Assume nothing

Be proactive and
find out

Caution flag! Too often students believe a topic has to look a particular way even if it doesn't seem or feel right. As a result, many students find themselves locked into a difficult position where the only way out is to try and force things to fit. Avoid this by doing what you think is right, and supporting your writing with research, etc.

WHAT DOES MY INSTRUCTOR EXPECT FROM ME?

Students often complain that they get an assignment from their instructor but are not told what the instructor expects from them. This usually shows up after an assignment is done with instructor comments like "This is not what the assignment was about." Or, "Why didn't you do this?"

Two things could be going on here. Either you misunderstood what the instructor was after, or, the instructor did not clarify what was wanted from the assignment.

How can you prevent this? The worst thing is to make assumptions about what you think your instructor intends. We all know the problems caused by wrong assumptions.

The answer is *be proactive*. If you're not certain what your instructor expects, ask. The best instructors encourage it.

A thesis tells your reader what you will argue in your paper.

Your argument is based on:

- Evidence you have gathered
- Research that points to a particular conclusion

Your success is a result of:

- Having a clear, forceful and supportable argument
- The ability to persuade your reader of the validity of that argument

STEP FOUR

identify your thesis

Your thesis is the key element upon which your essay or term paper is grounded. Without a solid, supportable thesis, the reader will question the work's validity.

So, *what is a thesis*?

DEFINITION:

A thesis is a guide for your reader. It tells your reader what you will argue in your paper. This argument is based on:

- Evidence you have gathered
- Research that points to a particular conclusion

Success is a result of:

1. Having a clear, forceful and supportable argument
2. Being able to persuade your reader of the validity of that argument.

The question to ask yourself, is therefore "Do I have a sound argument, backed by solid research, that I can present to my reader?"

Let me give you a couple of examples. The first is from Shakespeare's Hamlet. One of the critical debates has always revolved around Hamlet's sanity. Here's the thesis: *While Hamlet is tragically indecisive, my analysis shows that he is sane*. In my essay, I will explore Hamlet's initial encounter with his father's ghost, and his mistreatment of Ophelia. I will argue, based on my interpretation of these examples, that there is adequate evidence in the text to prove my claim that Hamlet is sane.

The case must be argued on the basis of the evidence in the text - not on your feelings about, in this case, the play. The reader asks "Show me the evidence to support your argument."

The second example comes from a more modern context. With the mapping of the human genome, companies have applied for thousands of gene patents. My thesis is that

Keep your thesis statement handy - where you can see it or find it - so you always remember your focus

If you are unable to prove your thesis, revise it, or reconsider it

patenting genes severely restricts basic research by universities and other public research institutions. I will argue that complex patent and licensing arrangements, now in place, prevent desirable research from being undertaken today and in the future.

My job is now to persuade you that a strong case exists for not accepting patents on genes.

Tips

We suggest that in your drafts (not your final copy) you keep emphasizing and reminding yourself of your thesis by underlining it in your introduction. If you cannot identify your thesis clearly, it is doubtful whether your reader will be able to do so either.

As well, consider writing your thesis in big letters and put it where you can see it. Take a copy of it in your binder when you're doing your research or writing, so you remember to stay on track.

Staying focused

Return to the thesis after writing each section to ensure that you are still on track. And, continue to argue your main point rather than drifting off on some tangent.

Keep asking yourself as you do additional research, "Is what I'm doing useful to my thesis?" If it isn't, either drop that point, or check to see if the thesis itself is valid.

Can you revise your thesis?

You are not obligated to stand by a thesis that cannot be proven. It may happen that as you go through various drafts, the evidence doesn't materialize, or draws you to a different conclusion. If this is the case, revise your thesis or reconsider it.

Summary

Your argument needs to be based on solid, factual support. Your empirical evidence can be a text, a report, a study, an article - but keep in mind that this evidence must persuade the reader to accept the validity of your position.

Research helps you to uncover your topic and provide evidence to support (or counter) your thesis

Be thorough in your research

Avoid handing in assignments that are:

- Thin on ideas and concepts
- Full of padding

STEP FIVE

do the research

There are three elements to this section on research:

1. *Why you do research and the sources available to you.*
2. A special section on *listening and speaking*, especially helpful for interviews and discussing your needs with resource people.
3. *Documentation* - how to document the sources you use.

WHY YOU DO RESEARCH

Research is carried out in order to find information about your topic so that you have solid material to support your ideas and arguments. What have others said about your topic? What new data exists? How will it support your point of view? Don't be surprised if what you find means that you'll have to shift the emphasis of your topic or thesis in some way.

Have I done enough research?

Instructors often complain that students don't take their research far enough. They base that opinion on assignments handed in that are "thin" or "skimpy" on ideas and concepts and full of "padding." Your objective is to make sure that in addition to your own thinking, class notes, etc., you do sufficient research for your assignment to be as thorough as possible.

In research there are ***primary*** *and* ***secondary*** *sources to go to for information:*

- Use the primary sources first
- Remember the importance of *diversity*. Information comes from a wide variety of sources

THE SOURCES

What sources do you use for your research? Here are some suggestions based on my own experience as well as advice from librarians.

Since the second edition of this booklet (1995), the Internet (the Net) has turned the world upside down. We can obtain information, immediately, from around the world. As a result, the Net is the source many of us turn to first. (Things are changing so fast that the Net increasingly gives access to CD-ROM and on line databases listed under primary sources.) I'll discuss the Net in a moment, but I want to caution you about using it as your primary source.

What I do suggest is the importance of diversity - carrying out research in many different areas. Information is not found in one place. It comes from a variety of sources, both primary and secondary:

Primary sources

- Library reference sections
  - encyclopedias, dictionaries, bibliographies
  - CD-ROM & on line databases
- Books
- Periodicals/journals
- People

Secondary sources

- The Internet
- Other networks

The primary sources to use first are:

- Library reference sections
- Books
- Periodicals/journals
- People

PRIMARY SOURCES

Library reference sections

In general it is faster and more efficient to use the focused indexes and catalogues provided in libraries to find both paper and automated material. The reference section contains a large amount of information to help you including encyclopedias, bibliographies and indexes to books and journals. There are also some very good automated databases (CD-ROM and on line).

Libraries are not the only places with reference sections. Material may also be available from corporations, governments and other organizations, such as newspapers, museums and archives.

Books

Your required course texts are major sources of information. The bibliographies in those texts may guide you to other useful material. You can also search in the library under the topic and see what other books are available.

Periodicals/journals

Periodicals/journals generally publish the most current thinking in a particular subject, discipline or activity. They add to the knowledge base of books and periodicals already published so they're very useful in acquiring the most up-to-date research.

Libraries carry periodical indexes, either printed or automated, that detail subject information, titles, authors, etc. Many also carry CD-ROM databases of the actual articles, often providing a summary of the information so you can determine if it's of value and worth reading the article itself.

For example, when I needed information on the impact of brand advertising from one country to another, accessing the word "brand" alone gave me hundreds of entries. Adding "international" to "brand" immediately limited the entries to ones that proved more fruitful.

People are often one of your best sources for information:

- Talk to librarians
- Consult instructors/ professors on campus or elsewhere
- Call an expert

Next, I was able to see a précis of each article to determine if it was worth reviewing and if it was available in the library.

You might want to check the latest journals in your areas of interest. I browse current journals for areas that interest me. It's amazing how often I find something I can use. Like playing a hunch, you develop a gut feel of where to look.

People

People can be one of your best sources for information. Using them well is a proactive step.

Librarians

In my experience librarians are invariably helpful and valuable. Not only can they assist you to find information more quickly, but more of it - from sources you probably never thought of, or had any idea existed.

Instructors/professors

Don't be afraid to ask your instructor/professor, or other instructors/professors on campus or elsewhere, who might point you in a direction, or give you advice to further your search.

Experts

Go to experts in the area you're writing about. If you're doing a piece on documentary film, talk to a local producer or director. If you're writing about an environmental issue, speak to someone in an environmental organization - or a company representative responsible for environmental issues. If you're writing about political or economic situations, consider speaking with a newspaper editor or reporter, or, depending on where you live, your local, regional or national politicians.

I find that people are almost always willing to help. Yes, sometimes they are too busy to talk; more likely, they simply haven't been asked. In my experience it almost always pays off. After all, they can only say "no."

When using the Internet, make sure that you:

- Focus on the information you need
- Obtain credible information
- Don't get sidetracked by interesting but unrelated web sites
- Give yourself a time limit

Print a copy of Internet/E-mail material

Web sites are constantly changing. We recommend that you take a print copy of any source material (Internet/E-mail) that you plan to use in your assignment. Then, if anyone asks, you can produce it.

SECONDARY SOURCES

The Internet

I want to caution you about using only the Internet. You will find excellent material, a lot of garbage and everything in between. Even with the best search engines, it isn't always easy to zero in on the material that you need. Librarians tell me that using the focused resources is much faster, and probably more reliable, than the Net.

Evaluate websites carefully. What are the credentials of the person(s) who set up the site? How often is it updated? Is the information complete or selected for a particular slant?

Don't get sidetracked using the Net. With its immense variety on sports, music, movies, games, books, sex, travel and everything else under the sun, the Net can easily take you off on a tangent. "Bookmark" an interesting site to check later, but not on your work schedule. Concentrate only on the research that applies to your topic. And "work your plan." In other words, stick to your time limit.

Keep a print copy of Net/E-mail material

I recommend that you print out a copy of anything from the Net (or E-mail) that you plan to use as a source, so that you can show it to someone if asked. The very nature of the World Wide Web is one of change. Organizations or individuals with web sites are expected to constantly update them, provide relevant information and delete dated material. As well, the site itself may no longer exist. A reference on its own, therefore, may not be the same, or even available.

E-mails also get deleted, or changed. A print copy is at least some proof.

Record your information carefully:

- For verification
- For documentation

Never plagiarize by passing off someone else's work as your own

Other networks

Many other databases are available, including those established by major newspapers such as The New York Times and The Globe & Mail. Access to major newspapers is readily available on the Net. I recently did some research on The Miami Circle, a unique archaeological find uncovered during excavation for a building site in downtown Miami. I was able to access pertinent articles from The Miami Herald via the Net.

Record information/credit sources

Take careful notes on where you found or received your information. It's all going to be important:

- If somebody asks you where it came from so they can check it
- To go down in your list of references, works cited, etc.

There's nothing worse than quoting something then being unable to recall where you found it, or who said it.

A note on plagiarism

Plagiarism is taking someone else's writing, music, artwork, etc. and passing it off as your own. There have been a number of court cases in recent years where the composer of a song has been accused of stealing the tune, or lyrics, from someone else. Some of the songs were hits so the amount of money involved was substantial.

More in keeping with what we're dealing with here, I know of a student who submitted a movie review as part of a class assignment. Well aware of the student's writing style, the teacher suspected something was wrong and checked the Net. Sure enough, the student had downloaded a review from a web site. Confronted, the student admitted what he'd done. It was a good lesson for everyone. Plagiarism leads to a failed grade.

SOME TIPS TO IMPROVE YOUR LISTENING AND SPEAKING

With listening, we often fail to give the speaker our full attention. That's because of the way we listen:

"We're either speaking or waiting to speak"

LISTENING & SPEAKING

Good listening and speaking skills will help you get the most out of working with library staff and doing interviews. They also help clarify the direction you're taking with your work.

Listening

How we listen makes a difference as to whether we receive and understand what someone else is trying to tell us. How many times have you been told "You didn't hear what I said?" Or "That's not what I meant." This happens because all too often we don't give the speaker ***our full attention.*** We get distracted. The problem is the way most of us listen:

"We're either speaking or waiting to speak."

Let me explain. When we listen to someone discuss something, especially if we disagree or want to make a point about what they're saying, we stop listening. Instead, we focus on what we want to say … we're waiting to speak. As often as not we'll interrupt the speaker with our point of view. We certainly won't catch the rest of what they have to say.

My point? If you're interviewing someone, if you're asking help from a librarian, listen to everything the other person has to say. If their viewpoint differs from yours, don't jump in to contradict it. Be curious instead. Explore the other person's perspective before you judge it. That way you'll hear and appreciate their overall point of view.

Assumptions can spell trouble:

"Did you really hear what you thought you heard?"

Check to find out

With speaking, make sure that you are:

- Clear on what you're after
- Proactive in achieving it

Beware - *assumptions* can spell trouble

A journalist interviews a well known public figure. After the interview is published, the individual complains to the editor about what was written. "That's not what I said. That's not what I meant. It's been taken out of context."

Did you hear what you thought you heard?

Too often we assume something means one thing, when in fact it means another. Or we jump to a conclusion without checking it out. What's the answer? Check your assumptions. If you interview people - reporters, business people, civic officials, social advocates, whoever - listen to what they have to say, then *summarize* what you think you heard. They'll tell you if you're accurate or not.

Speaking

When you speak, your intention is to communicate something to another person so that they understand what you have said, and if necessary, respond. In terms of speaking with librarians, or interviewing people, two elements will be helpful to you:

- Be clear about what you want
- Be proactive

Be clear about what you want

Know what it is you're after. It's useful to prepare yourself by creating an agenda with a series of questions for which you need answers. At the same time, be prepared to explain what it is you're doing and what you hope to achieve. That gives people a better idea of what you need and therefore how best to help you.

Be proactive in contacting those who can make a difference, or contribution, to your knowledge and efforts

Document your sources

- To acknowledge the source
- To register where the source may be located

Be proactive

Many people miss out on obtaining valuable information because they're scared to contact someone or some organization. I appreciate that this can be intimidating. The proactive step, however, is to make the call. In my experience the results are invariably positive. People like to be asked for help and advice.

Summary

Listening and speaking are skills that make a difference in your ability to communicate and receive communication from others. Improving and applying these skills will absolutely help you in your research. It will also contribute in every area of life.

DOCUMENTATION

Documenting your sources is an essential element of writing essays, term papers and many other kinds of reports and submissions. There are two reasons for documentation:

1. To acknowledge the source - i.e. give credit to an author, an organization, etc.
2. To register where the source was located - whether a book, a periodical, an interview, the Internet, etc., so that if someone wishes to verify that source, they know where to find it

Giving credit to the source is pretty basic. Including the source in a list of references is more complex. It's not made easier by having several different systems, such as MLA, APA, Chicago, etc., each with its own distinctive style. What is important is that you be consistent in the system you use.

Choose the appropriate documentation style and apply it consistently

NOTE: Be aware that with the massive changes in electronic communications, documentation of electronic references is in process and subject to interpretation. Simply try to be consistent in how you apply it.

In this booklet we'll compare the two styles most commonly used - MLA (Modern Language Association) and APA (American Psychological Association), and we'll deal only with the list of references at the end of your essay or term paper. These references are both print and electronic. In MLA style the list is called "Works Cited"; in APA style it is called "References."

Both MLA and APA require that all references:

- *Are double spaced* (To save space in this booklet, all examples are single spaced.)
- *Use a hanging indent*; i.e. the first line of a reference is flush left with subsequent lines indented.

Which style should you use?

When do you use the MLA and when do you use the APA? Generally speaking, MLA style is used in English and the humanities. APA style is used in the social sciences. If in doubt, ask your instructor.

APA - Update

In 2001, the APA published the fifth edition of its Publication Manual. Among the changes in referencing was the replacement of underlining with *italics*. Other changes included the shortening of the "retrieval statement" for electronic references. These changes have been reflected in the examples that follow.

Documentation of electronic references

Guidelines for referencing electronic sources is clearer than in April 2000 when the third edition of this booklet was published. Nonetheless, it still appears likely that further changes will take place over the next few years. Be consistent in how you record the references you use and check APA and MLA web sites for more information or answers to your questions.

Summary

Our intention is that the comparisons between MLA and APA on pages 70 through 81 will help you document your reference sources, both print and electronic, more easily.

MLA

General Rules

With the author, MLA lists the last name and first name as follows:

`Johnston, Heather.`
[Use initials if first name not known]

With the title, MLA capitalizes the first letter of major words and proper nouns.

`Do You Know the Way to San Jose?`

With the date:
- MLA places the date at the end, or next to the end
- May, June & July are spelled in full. Abbreviate all others: e.g. Dec. Sept.
- The date sequence is day month year with no commas:

  `1 Jan. 2000`

With the place of publication, unless the city is well known - e.g. Montreal - add the state or province (abbreviated - ON, TX, BC, NY), or name of the country.

If references overlap a line, indent each
additional line by 5 spaces or 1/2 inch.

Books

- Last name, first name of author.
- Title.
- Place of publication: publisher, year of publication.

```
Millman, Dan. Way of the Peaceful Warrior.
    Tiburon, CA: H.J. Kramer, 1984.
```

APA

General Rules

With the author, APA lists the last name followed by initial(s).

`Johnston, H.L.`

With the title, APA capitalizes only the first letter of the first word, proper nouns and the first word after a colon.

`Do you know the way to San Jose?`

With the date:

- APA always places the date of publication second, in parentheses after the author's name.
- Months are spelled in full - i.e. April, December
- The date sequence is generally year, month day:

  `2000, January 1`
- If no date is available, write: (n.d.).

With the place of publication, unless the city is well known - e.g. Montreal - add the state or province (abbreviated - ON, TX, BC, NY), or name of the country.

If references overlap a line, indent each
additional line by 5 spaces or 1/2 inch.

Books

- Last name, initial(s) of author.
- (Year of publication).
- *Title.*
- Place of publication: publisher.

Millman, D. (1984). *Way of the peaceful warrior.* Tiburon, CA: H.J. Kramer.

MLA

More than one author:

- For first author: Name, first name,
- For additional authors: first name last name, (*normally use comma before "and"*)
- Use "and" in full

Connors, Roger, Tom Smith, and Craig Hickman. The Oz Principle. Etc...

More than three authors:

- First named author is listed followed by "et al." ("et al." refers to the Latin "and others"). If there were a fourth author to The Oz Principle, the reference would begin:

Connors, Roger, et al.

Journals/periodicals

- Last name, first name of author.
- "Title of article."
- Name of publisher/publication:
  a. Monthly magazine: Publisher/publication.
  b. Weekly magazine & newspaper: Publisher/publication (no period)
  c. Journal paginated by volume/issue: Publisher/publication volume #. issue # (e.g. Volume 22 Issue 7 = 22.7)
- Date:
  a. Monthly magazine: Month year:
  b. Weekly magazine & newspaper: Day month year:
  c. Journal paginated by volume/issue: (Year):
- Page #s: 333-334.

Article in a monthly magazine

Muoio, Anna. "Mint Condition." Fast Company. Dec. 1999: 330-348.

APA

More than one author:

- Name, initial(s)., separated by commas.
- Use "&" abbreviation instead of the word "and"

Connors, R., Smith, T., & Hickman, C. (1994).
    The Oz principle. Etc...

More than three authors:

- All author names are listed unless there are six or more when it would go to:

Connors, R., et al.

Journals/periodicals

- Last name, initial(s) of author.
- Date:
  a. Monthly magazine: (Year, month).
  b. Weekly magazine & newspaper:
     (Year, month day).
  c. Journal paginated by volume/issue: (Year).
- Title of article.
- Name of publisher/publication:
  a. Monthly/weekly magazine and newspaper:
     Publisher/publication, [Note: comma italicized]
  b. Journal paginated by volume/issue:
     Publisher/publication, volume # (issue #),
     (e.g. Volume 22 Issue 7 = 22 (7),) [Note: italicize only volume number, not issue number]
- Page #s: 333-334.
  [Except for newspapers & magazines, in which case the page numbers in your reference are preceded by 'p.' or 'pp.']

Article in a monthly magazine

Muoio, A. (1999, December). Mint condition.
    Fast Company, pp. 330-348.

MLA

Article in a weekly magazine

Schneider, Peter. "A German Leftist Who Loves to Count Beans." The New York Times Magazine 13 Sept. 1998: 60-63.

Article in a newspaper

Scoffield, Heather. "Safety Activists Want Labels for Modified Foods." The Globe and Mail 10 July 1999: A5.

Article in a journal paginated by volume

Boesch, Christophe, and Michael Tomasello. "Chimpanzee and Human Cultures." Cultural Anthropology 39 (1998): 591-614.

Article in a journal paginated by issue

Segal, Gerald. "China's Changing Shape." Foreign Affairs 73.3 (1994): 43-58.

Video

View from the Typewriter. Prod. Robert Duncan, George Johnson. National Film Board of Canada, 1993.

Motion Picture

The Indian in the Cupboard. Dir. Frank Oz. Prods. Kathleen Kennedy, Frank Marshall and Jane Startz. Columbia Pictures, 1995.

Personal interview

- Last name, first name.
- Type of communication.
- Date: Day month year.
- Each section is separated by periods.

Bettman, Erica. Personal Interview at Miami Airport. 17 July 1997.

APA

Article in a weekly magazine

Schneider, P. (1998, September 13). A German leftist who loves to count beans. *The New York Times Magazine,* pp. 60-63.

Article in a newspaper

Scoffield, H. (1999, July 10). Safety activists want labels for modified foods. *The Globe and Mail,* p. A5.

Article in a journal paginated by volume

Boesche, C. & Tomasello, M. (1998). Chimpanzee and human cultures. *Current Anthropology, 39,* 591-614.

Article in a journal paginated by issue

Segal, G. (1994). China's changing shape. *Foreign Affairs, 73* (3), 43-58.

Video

Duncan, R. & Johnson, G. (Producers). (1993). *View from the typewriter* [Videorecording]. Montreal: National Film Board of Canada.

Motion Picture

Kennedy, K., Marshall, F. & Startz, J. (Producers), & Oz, F. (Director). (1995). *The Indian in the cupboard* [Motion picture]. United States: Columbia Pictures.

Personal interview

The APA Manual states that personal communications, such as an interview, should be cited in text only. This also applies to E-mail - see page 81.

MLA

A World Wide Web site

Include as much of the following as possible:

- Name of author, editor, compiler, etc., (if known): Last name, first name.
- "Title of document or portion." (If relevant)
- Title of web site.
- Date of web site, if known—or latest update: day month year.
- Name of any institution/organization sponsoring the site.
- Date of access: day month year
- <URL>. [Note: period outside angle bracket at end of URL]
- Where possible keep the URL on one line or break it in a logical place.

"Feminism in Jane Austen." Pride and Prejudice-Notes on Education, Marriage, Status of Women, etc. 11 Nov. 1999. The Republic of Pemberley. 5 Dec. 1999 <http://www.pemberley.com/janeinfo/pptopic2.html>.

(To minimize complexity, we have not included statement of length [for example, number of paragraphs] for regular web site. You may include if you wish to do so, but be consistent.)

APA

A World Wide Web site

Include as much of the following as possible:
- Name of author, editor, compiler, etc., (if known): Last name, initial(s).
- Date of web site, if known - or latest update. (Month day, year).
- Title of document or portion (if relevant). *
- *Title of web site.*
- Retrieval statement including date of access - month day, year - and URL [Note: change in date sequence + no period at end of URL]
- Where possible keep the URL on one line or break it in a logical place

Feminism in Jane Austen. (1999, November 11). *Pride and Prejudice–Notes on Education, Marriage, Status of Women, etc.* Retrieved December 5, 1999 from http://www.pemberley.com/janeinfo/pptopic2.html

* If author not known, open with title, followed by date, as in the example above.

MLA

Article from a publication on the World Wide Web

Include as much of the following as possible:

- Name of author (if known): Last name, first name.
- "Title of Article."
- Name of publication
- Volume #. Issue # or other identifying number (if given)
- Date of publication: *as per print style:*
- Number range or total number of pages or paragraphs, if they are numbered.
- Date of access <URL>.

Stanwood, P.G. "Affliction and Flight in Herbert's Poetry: A Note." Early Modern Literary Studies 1.2 (1995): paragraphs 1-11. 6 Dec. 1999 <http://unixg.ub.ca:7001/0/e-sources/emls/01-2/stanherb.html>.

APA

Article from a publication on the World Wide Web

References begin with the same information as would be provided for a printed source. Then the web information is placed in a retrieval statement at the end of the reference.

- Name of author: Last name, initial(s).
- Date of publication. (Year, Month)
- Title of article.
- *Title of publication, volume #* (issue #)
- Retrieval statement including date of access and URL [Note: no period at end of URL]

Stanwood, P.G. (1995). Affliction and flight in Herbert's poetry: A note. *Early Modern Literary Studies, 1* (2). Retrieved December 6, 1999 from http://unixg.ub.ca:7001/0/e-sources/emls/01-2/stanherb.html

You would reference as indicated above if you believed that the electronic article was different from the print version. If, however, it was simply a duplicate of the print version, all you need note is that you used the electronic version.

Stanwood, P.G. (1995). Affliction and flight in Herbert's poetry: A note [Electronic version]. *Early Modern Literary Studies, 1* (2).

MLA

Article from a CD-ROM database

Include as much of the following as possible:

- Name of author (if known): Last name, first name.
- "Title of Article."
- Title of Printed Source
- Volume #. Issue # (if given)
- Date of printed source: *as per print style.*
- Page reference for printed source (if given).
- Title of Database.
- Medium (CD-ROM).
- Name of CD-ROM source.
- Electronic publication date (if noted): Month year.

Reynolds, C.V. "3500 B.C. – A Very Good Year." Discover 13.1 (1992): 60. Academic Search Elite. CD-ROM. EBSCO.

E-mail

- Name of originator: last name, first name.
- Title of communication, if available:
  a. "Subject line from posting," or,
  b. "Description of document."
- E-mail to recipient.
- Date: day month year.

Sawers, Neil. "Plans for the Millennium." Personal E-mail to Liz Whitney. 28 Oct. 1999.

APA

Article from a CD-ROM Database

After reference information that would be included for a print source, add a retrieval statement to the reference.

- Name of author: Last name, initial(s).
- Date of printed source: *as per print style.*
- Title of article.
- *Title of printed source.*
- Page reference for printed source (if given).
- Retrieval statement including date of access and name of database.

Reynolds, C.V. (1992). 3500 B.C. – A very good year. *Discover, 13* (1), 60. Retrieved January 17, 2000, from EBSCO database.

E-mail

APA requires personal communications, such as E-mails, to be cited in text only since they do not provide recoverable data.

Organizing your work/having a good outline, pulls everything together so that you can write logically from start to finish

To create it:

1. Decide which approach to use to build your case
2. Pull the information together in a logical, step by step format

STEP SIX

develop the organization/outline

6

INTRODUCTION

You've got your topic and you know what you want to prove about it. Now you have to organize it in a logical, step-by-step structure that leads from opening paragraph to conclusion. Some call this an outline; others, simply organizing your work. It is a product of:

- Your topic/thesis
- Your research
- Your class notes
- Your own thinking

With a good organization or outline:

- You're clear how your assignment hangs together from beginning to end
- The first draft is easier to write
- You are less likely to encounter writer's block

To create your organization or outline, you must:

1. Decide which approach to use to build your case
2. Pull the information together in a logical, step by step format

DECIDE WHICH APPROACH TO USE TO BUILD YOUR CASE

There are a number of approaches that can be taken to build a case. The most frequently used are:

- Descriptive
- Chronological
- Comparative
- Build to a climax

Which is the best approach to use in building your case?

Is it *descriptive*?

Is it *chronological*?

Is it *comparative*?

Is it *build to a climax*?

Descriptive

You're asked to describe something. With this approach you bring forward:

- Your specific viewpoint
- The viewpoints of others
- The merits of each point of view
- Your conclusions

Chronological

You talk about the sequence of events. For example, if your topic was the UN decision to hold an election for independence in East Timor, describe:

- Each event that led up to that decision, identifying the date/time that it happened
- The impact of the event in forwarding the action
- Your and others' interpretation of the event's importance
- Your conclusions

Comparative

Use a comparative approach if asked to compare or contrast one system with another:

- Comparing occurs between the same things. For example, apples and apples
- Contrasting occurs between two different things. For example, apples and oranges
- Your conclusions

Build to a climax

Take your topic and build to your climax:

- Begin with the least important steps
- Add progressively bigger steps, each building on the previous step
- End with the climactic step, built upon those that have gone before and leading to your conclusions. For example, in preparing to run a marathon you start with short training runs, add in longer endurance runs, and end with the climactic step itself: the big race.

The best approach may in fact be a *combination* of approaches

How should you create the logical sequence for writing the draft?

You could do it:

- In your head
- By creating lists
- By using index cards

Reality: Combining different approaches

Usually one approach will be combined with elements of another. For example, a chronological story can easily build to a climax, each event getting bigger and bigger, as in the marathon cited in "Build to a climax."

PULL THE INFORMATION TOGETHER IN A LOGICAL, STEP-BY-STEP FORMAT

Once you have decided which approach to use, assemble all the information you've gathered into the step-by-step, linear format the essay or term paper requires. This sequencing builds your case and supporting arguments from introduction to conclusion.

For some, this step-by-step format is a very formal outline. For others it's less formal and more loosely organized. There is no right or wrong way to do this. The only thing you must do is have a logical sequence that goes down on paper.

How to create the logical sequence

In your head. Some people, especially if it's a short essay, simply do it in their head.

Write out a list. List everything down on a piece of paper, from class notes to class texts and research. You might number the items, moving them around as needed to develop a logical sequence.

Use index cards. Each item goes down on an index card. You can color code items by topic sub categories or use different colored cards.

You next sort the cards to sequence them and then number them. It's easy enough to lay cards out on a table - or the floor - and move them around into the desired sequence.

- By using a database
- By employing mind map techniques

Lay out the basic structure:

- Opening section
- Main body (2-4 sections)
- Conclusion

Use a database. A computer database is another way in which you can first store information, sort it and arrange it in sequence for writing. This is particularly suitable for a major term paper requiring storage of a lot of information.

Use mind map or similar techniques. Making use of a mind map or sticky notes system is a great way to organize your information. For example, the seven priorities established in the analysis of "Health Care in a developing world," is ideal for the writing sequence.

POST SEQUENCE - LAY OUT THE BASIC STRUCTURE

Once you have your sequence, you can lay out the basic structure (often done simultaneously with the sequence). The structure consists of the various blocks that make up the essay or term paper. They are:

- An introduction/opening section
- Main body
- Summary or conclusion

Introduction/Opening Section

In this section you introduce your topic, give some background and what you intend to prove (your thesis). Depending on the length or complexity of your work, this could be as little as a single paragraph - or multiple paragraphs over several pages.

Allocate a section for each major argument or concept

Use sticky notes or index cards to help you

Main Body

The main body follows the introduction. How long is it? That depends on the number of major arguments, ideas, concepts you plan to introduce and the amount of material to support them. Some suggest that it be from two to four sections.

Allocate a section to each major argument or concept you plan to discuss. Break that up into the number of paragraphs required by the argument. It might only be a couple of paragraphs. It could be as many as a dozen or more.

In laying out your headings, check to make sure that they flow from one part into another. If they don't, move your information around until they do.

If you use sticky notes or index cards, they're easy to move around until the sequence/structure works for you. Your goal is to create flow - where the conclusions of one paragraph lead or bridge to the next paragraph or section.

Conclusion

The conclusion is the final section. The objective is to set out your conclusions in such a way as to prove your thesis. The length depends on the amount of material you have to cover. It could be no more than a couple of paragraphs. If there are a dozen key points you need to summarize, then the paragraph count will go up.

In Step 8, "Complete the first draft," we'll go into more detail on the development of the structure.

TIPS

- Treat every argument fully, regardless of how short or how weak it may appear

- In your work, you may wish to consider going from general to specific

When you've completed your organization or outline, ask yourself:

- Does everything relate to my thesis?
- Does it flow?

TIPS FOR ORGANIZING YOUR WORK

Treat each argument comprehensively and thoroughly

Just because one argument is shorter than another, or seemingly less important, still treat it fully. Build your case, however, by starting with weaker arguments and adding stronger and stronger ones.

Go from general to specific

In discussing Step 3, "Come up with the right topic," I spoke of the value of limiting the topic by going from general to specific. In organizing your work it may also help to go from general to specific.

Suppose your outline involves the average number of hours children watch television per week. You could:

- Begin in *general* terms
- Zero in on a *specific* factor

For example, a general factor might be that

> *"more and more parents are concerned that their children are watching too much television."*

This could lead to a specific factor such as

> *"the need to prevent children from watching programs that contain violence."*

COMPLETING YOUR ORGANIZATION/OUTLINE

Once you've completed your organization or outline, go through it and ask yourself:

- Does each section relate to my thesis?
- Does each section flow from beginning to end, point by point, argument by argument, paragraph by paragraph?

If you're well organized, whether in outline form or some other structure, writing the actual draft will prove much easier to accomplish.

Write with your reader in mind

(Step 7)

Complete the first draft

(Step 8)

Revise and edit the draft

(Step 9)

Take one last look

(Step 10)

THE WRITING STEPS

There are four Writing Steps. They are:

- **Write with your reader in mind**
- **Complete the first draft**
- **Revise and edit the draft**
- **Take one last look**

Step 7 often gets overlooked. A screenwriter writes for the movie audience. A sports reporter writes for sports fans. You are writing for your professor, instructor, lecturer, board of examiners, etc. It's very important to keep the specific audience in mind from the start. If you know them well and are aware of what they are expecting, tailor your topic, and how you present it, to that audience.

Steps 8 and 9 logically follow one another. First you write the draft, then revise the content as necessary. Finally you polish the revised draft through editing and proofreading.

Step 10 is the pause before handing in your work. It's that last chance to step back and think about what you've created. Are you happy with it? Should any final changes be made?

Put yourself in your reader's shoes so as to understand who they are

Think about what your reader expects from you

STEP SEVEN

write with your reader in mind

7

WHO IS YOUR READER?

In business, one of the things you have to learn is to put yourself in your customer's shoes. If literally you sell sports shoes, and a customer wants a pair of runners, you'll ask questions like what kind of running, how many miles, what kind of terrain, how much support, weight of the shoe, etc., as well as price.

Start thinking about your readers in that way. Put yourself in their shoes. Who are they? Is your reader your instructor, or is it someone else? What do you know about them, their thinking, their expectations, that would help you write with them in mind?

WHAT YOUR READER EXPECTS FROM YOU

Your reader wants to know that you can take a topic and, through your writing, show that you:

- Fully understand and can think about it
- Have done the required research, identified other points of view and can discuss each of them
- Are able to use the evidence you gathered through your studies, research, etc., to convincingly present your arguments
- Can express and justify your own view in light of the opinion of others, including that of your reader
- Are able to write in a manner that reflects the language, tone and professional discipline of your area of study

Think about what you want your reader to remember from your work

Get feedback from others to see if what you've written will work for your reader

WHAT YOU WANT YOUR READER TO REMEMBER

- That you set up your thesis and proved it
- That you explained what had to be explained, avoiding assumptions
- That you were effective at using the evidence you found to construct your arguments clearly and concisely
- That your own opinions and conclusions were expressed
- The two or three major points you made, even when the detail of your work has been forgotten

Test drive what you write

Before you hand in your work, try it on for size with someone else - preferably an independent reader who has no vested interest in you one way or another. Friends may work, as may parents, provided they're willing to be honest. What you're looking for is feedback. Does what I've written work for my audience? Does it flow? Are assumptions or quantum leaps being made? Are there holes big enough to drive a truck through?

This kind of rehearsal is extremely valuable, if you're willing and have the time to do it. It invariably makes for a better final product *focused on the reader.*

Always work from your organization/outline and thesis

Use wide margins & double spacing

Begin with the basics:

1. Introduce the topic
2. Give some background
3. What you intend to prove (your thesis statement)

So you're blocked. Now what?

- you may need to take a break
- you may need to talk to someone

STEP EIGHT

complete the first draft

8

Your work is organized/outlined. You have your thesis. You're ready to begin the first draft.

As you write, *keep checking your organization/outline and thesis to make sure you're on track.*

Give yourself plenty of space on each page to make corrections. I recommend at least a three inch margin, plus double or triple spacing.

HOW TO BEGIN

Introducing the topic

The first thing we normally do is introduce the topic, give some background/history about it, why that particular topic was chosen and what we intend to prove about it (thesis).

Now - one of the things we all like to do is come up with a dynamite opening paragraph. Sometimes we can produce it right off the top. We get the correct phrasing, or the analogy is perfect, or it just works. Too often, however, we try for a winning paragraph and however hard we try, nothing works. We keep struggling because the opening is important. It sets the tone. But right now, especially if we're blocked, it's not what counts.

What to do if you're blocked

If it's not an essay in class and you're at home, maybe you need to take a break and do something else. If you're not in an exam room, you might talk to a friend or your instructor. They may have some insights for you.

Writing strategies if blocked

(especially by that opening paragraph)

- Write the basics
- Jump into what you know (part of the middle section, whatever) as long as you keep going
- Do the end notes and bibliography

You can always return to the opening paragraph, or wherever else you were blocked, later on

But what if you are in an exam room, or it's midnight and the essay has to be handed in at ten the next morning? Here are some suggestions on how to proceed:

Write the basic information

Don't attempt a "winning" paragraph for the moment. Instead, keep it simple. Just write the basic information your reader needs to know: what your topic is about and what you intend to prove. "My topic is about Hamlet's state of mind and I intend to prove, through my research and my analysis of Shakespeare's text, that he was sane."

You can always return to the opening paragraph later, when more of the writing is under your belt. At that time, you might want to think like an ad copywriter:

"How can I 'hook' my readers so that they're intrigued by what I have to say and want to read on?"

The hook may give you an interesting lead in - even a provocative one.

Jump into what you do know

Another thing you could do is jump into what you do know. If you're confident about those middle paragraphs, start working with them. That still keeps you moving forward. You can go back and make the connections to the opening paragraph later.

Do the end notes and bibliography

Get the end notes and bibliography out of the way so that you don't have to think about them on completing your assignment.

For each main body section argument/idea:

- Present idea/concept
- Debate it
- Draw your conclusion
- Bridge to the text

Paragraphs may consist of a few sentences, or several, depending on complexity

Each sentence must move the "action" forward & relate to each other

BEYOND THE OPENING PARAGRAPH

Writing the main sections

Once the opening paragraph or paragraphs are done you proceed to write the two to four sections that contain the major arguments, concepts and ideas to support your thesis. These sections consist of a single paragraph or a series of paragraphs.

Each section deals with a new idea or concept from your organization/outline. Your job is to develop and work your descriptions and arguments concerning this idea or concept through to completion. The sequence is:

- Present the idea/concept
- Debate the pros and cons
- Draw your conclusions
- Bridge or transition to the next section/paragraph

Paragraphs & sentences - your building blocks

A paragraph may be as few as three or four sentences to as many as ten or fifteen. Use as many sentences as you need to illustrate the idea/concept.

The first sentence in a paragraph introduces the second. The second refers back to the first and introduces the third and so on. These sentences provide full or sustained development. It's like a knit pattern. If it doesn't connect, it will unravel and the reader won't be able to progress "with you." *(You want the reader to follow what you've said and understand it the first time around, effortlessly.)*

Finally you have a sentence, or sentences, which create "closure" for that paragraph as well as being the hook to the next paragraph and a bridge or transition to the next idea/concept.

Each section must be complete in itself

TIPS

- Let your writing flow
- Stay focused
- Keep checking your outline and thesis
- Remember your reader

If you're writing a business essay instead of an academic subject, I suggest that you avoid overly long paragraphs. It's often easier to get your point across with a fresh paragraph than to make an existing paragraph too long or complex. This may also be valid for academic purposes.

Make sure each section is complete in itself

Each section you write must be complete in itself. Key ideas and arguments are always presented and debated, and conclusions are drawn. It's important, however, that you show your reader how these conclusions lead or bridge naturally to the next idea in your organization/outline. This becomes the next section ... and so on.

OTHER USEFUL TIPS

Let the writing flow

In this first cut at your work, minimize editing. Too much editing impedes flow and tends to hinder progress. It's more important to get your ideas down on paper so you can examine them and play around with them. Don't worry if you write too much. You can always revise or edit later.

Stay focused

Keep checking your outline and thesis

Don't forget your reader

Can your reader follow your arguments, descriptions, analysis and conclusions? If not, what might you have to change?

TIPS

- Apply the K.I.S.S. principle to help keep writing clear and easily understood

- Fully develop what you're working on:
  - complete the discovery process
  - do enough research
  - avoid writing based on skimpy material, irrelevant material, or duplication

- Beware of jargon

Remember the K.I.S.S. principle

The K.I.S.S. principle stands for "Keep It Simple, Students!" Though more of a business term, the K.I.S.S. principle can be very useful in writing, especially if you're writing about topics that deal with business or the economy.

The rationale behind the K.I.S.S. principle is that we often make things more complicated than they need to be. In our writing that can mean:

- Explanations that are too intricate and long-winded
- Sentences that are overly long and complex

If you can construct your arguments simply and clearly, using less words rather than more and shorter sentences rather than longer ones, they're often easier to follow and more likely to the understood and remembered.

The opposite to K.I.S.S. may also be true

Academic writing tends to follow more complex patterns than writing for business. Instructors are often concerned that students stop the discovery process too soon and don't fully develop what they're working on. This is particularly true with research. Too many students write a 2,000 word essay on skimpy material. Because they haven't done enough research they try to fudge through it, duplicating what they've said and filling in with irrelevant material.

The message? Do the "up front" work necessary to uncover solid material, ideas and arguments to support what you're saying.

Inappropriate jargon

Use the specific language of a discipline if that's your area of study and your reader is familiar with it. Otherwise it comes across as jargon, or worse, talking down. Based on the K.I.S.S. principle, avoid it.

When you reach your conclusions, ask yourself:

- Does everything flow?
- Does it support my thesis?

Make sure the conclusions you draw are your own

Consider linking your conclusions back to the opening paragraph

REACHING CONCLUSIONS

All your ideas, descriptions and arguments are down on paper. You're about to write your final paragraph. Ask yourself:

- Does everything I've written flow logically to this point?
- Does it support my thesis?

Your overall conclusions are built step by step on the conclusions derived from each individual section. It may support your thesis to restate these individual section findings prior to setting down your overall conclusions.

Make sure that the conclusions are yours, not somebody else's (even though others may agree with you). You want your reader to know that they've been reached based on your classwork, your research, your studies and, above all, your own thinking.

Link back to your opening paragraph

I like to tie my conclusions back to the statements made in the opening paragraph. For me, it connects the beginning and the end, making the work whole and complete. For example, let's say your topic was about the impact of television on children. In your introduction you said, "When I was a kid, my parents allowed us to watch anything as long as we were in bed by eight-thirty."

Based on your findings that unsupervised television watching leads to undesirable attitudes or exposure to impressionable images, you might conclude that "I wish my parents had done things differently. I recommend that today's parents exhibit greater care in what they allow their children to watch." This connects the beginning of your work with the end.

If your thesis does not work, re-evaluate it

When you've finished writing:

- Read what you've written out loud
- Note where major changes may be required
- Make minor changes (if easy to do)
- Set the draft aside and return to it later. This often gives you a fresh perspective on what you've written.

What if your thesis doesn't pan out?

Any time you realize that your thesis won't work, stop and see what will. An unworkable thesis has no value. Not only will your grades suffer, but so will your self-esteem. Even though it means extra work, take the proactive step and rework it.

YOUR CONCLUSIONS ARE WRITTEN. NOW WHAT?

You've put your pen down. You've hit "save" for the last time. What's next?

Read what you've written out loud

Reading out loud gives you a sense of how well your essay or term paper works. It will also tell you where changes are required. (Step 9 details the benefits of reading out loud.) If you're not good at reading out loud, get someone else to do it while you listen.

Mark on the draft where major reworking or additional input is required, or where something needs to be deleted.

Consider making minor changes as part of the first draft rather than leaving them for the revision stage.

Once you've made any initial changes, set the draft aside. If you can leave it for a day or two, you can come back to it refreshed. You might also want to discuss your efforts with friends, or in a writing lab in order to get additional feedback.

First revise the content,
then edit what
you've written

STEP NINE

revise and edit the draft

9

Writers often say that "writing" is "rewriting." My experience is that the more "up front" work you do in the Clarifying Steps, the less rewriting or revision your work will require. That's the payoff for all the pre-writing, research and topic exploration.

STEP 9 HAS TWO PARTS... REVISION AND EDITING.

1. ***Revision*** comes first and deals with content. What do you need to change about the content? There are a number of reasons for this:

- You have new information to incorporate
- Old information is not relevant and should be deleted
- Your understanding of a situation changes and the writing needs to reflect it. (This might include a change in your thesis.)
- The sequencing of what you've written doesn't work and has to be altered

2. ***Editing and proofreading*** follows revision. This is where you deal with the style and tone of what you've written. You change words and phrases, and shift things around to fit better. It doesn't alter the content. The result is a work more clearly and fluidly written, so that the reader can fully understand and appreciate what you're trying to say and prove.

(When you revise, you're also editing so there's no hard and fast rule here. However, once revision is complete, focus on the editing.)

Reading out loud helps answer key questions:

- Is anything missing?
- Does the overall impression work?
- Is the work focused and on track?
- Are sections complete in themselves?
- Does it flow?

Why you should read your work out loud

There are good reasons to read your work out loud - whether you read it yourself (some people like to tape themselves and play it back), or have someone else read it to you:

- ***You won't miss anything.*** Reading to yourself, it's easy to miss a "left out" word, incorrect use of grammar, a sentence without a verb, etc. Reading out loud usually picks up these errors.

- ***It gives you some idea of whether your work hangs together or not.*** It tells you if something's missing in the content. Are there unexplained gaps? Are there unproved assumptions? Is the reader asked to accept giant leaps of faith? All these get flagged as areas to work on.

- ***It gives you an overall impression of your essay or term paper*** - where it works, where it doesn't and where you need to spend more time.

- ***It tells you if your work is focused and on track.*** Does everything you've written pertain to your thesis? Where it doesn't, mark it for further attention.

- ***It helps you assess if each section produces a cogent argument or description.*** Is each section complete in itself? If not, what must you do to change and/or improve it?

- ***It tells you if your writing flows.*** Does one sentence flow to the next? Does one paragraph lead to another? If the paragraphs don't connect, what kind of bridge is required to join them? Is a word, a phrase, sentence, or paragraph in the wrong place? Is something missing entirely?

More reasons for reading out loud:

- Have you repeated yourself?
- Is the tone consistent?
- Did you avoid jargon?
- Did you avoid junk or garbage?
- Does it stimulate the desire to read on?

- ***You know if you've repeated yourself.*** Is what you've said redundant? Have you used the same word or phrasing too often, or one right after the other?

- ***Consistency of tone.*** Is the tone used throughout your work consistent, and will it appeal to your reader? Reading out loud identifies where the tone is off.

- ***You avoid junk or garbage.*** When you read what you've written, keep your "junk meter" on. What do I mean by that? Imagine that you have a mental junk meter that goes off whenever you hear the following:

  - gross generalizations
  - assumptions that can't be proven
  - excessive wordiness
  - writing that sounds great but has little or nothing to do with the topic

  As you read, ask yourself "Does this thought, this paragraph, this word belong in my work? Is it junk? Is it garbage?" If you have any doubts, strike it out!

- ***It brings your work off the page.*** Does your work come alive when read? Can you "feel" it? Does it draw some kind of emotional response?

  The best writing comes alive because it's written in a way that doesn't leave the work too dry and flat:

  - it sounds right
  - it has energy
  - it flows
  - it stimulates

  Your style, the words and phrases you use, and the compelling quality of your arguments all have a lot to do with it. Do these elements inform the reader? Do they stimulate the desire to read on?

Make a back-up copy of your work

When revising/editing:

1. Complete printout
2. General revision of whole document or in chunks
3. Input changes, and do another printout
4. Revise/edit, input changes and give yourself a new printout until satisfied

FINAL POINTS

Once you have highlighted the areas for revision, rework your text until you're satisfied with the content and the arguments you've put together to support your thesis.

When revision is done, edit your work. Follow the recommendations we've already made concerning tone, flow, language, etc.

COMPUTERS

When using computers, obey the following rule:

"Always make a backup copy of your work."

In revising and editing, some of us edit directly on screen. I prefer to give myself a printout from which to work. In my experience, this is a good way to proceed:

1. Once you've written your draft, give yourself a printout.
2. Read it, then revise/edit the printout. Here's where wide margins and double/triple spacing really help. Not only do I rewrite but there are arrows all over the place where I want something inserted, or sentences and paragraphs put in a different place.
3. You can revise/edit the whole printout, or, do it in sections. If it's short, like a letter, do it in one pass. If there are several sections, I often revise/edit each section on its own - which makes the revisions extremely manageable.
4. Input changes, give yourself another printout, read and revise as necessary until you're satisfied that your work is complete.

Spellcheck...

- Won't pick up everything
- Won't check your punctuation

Reading out loud helps correct spelling, punctuation and grammar

"Spellcheck" on your computer

Spellcheck helps proof your spelling. However it won't pick up the error if you've typed "the" where you meant to say "they." Reading out loud will do that.

Spellcheck won't detect your use of "whose" instead of "who's" either. For this kind of error and for mistakes in punctuation, you'll need to examine your text more closely.

You may want to run your work through a grammar checker. These programs can be useful in assessing such factors as correct use of grammar or proper sentence construction. Like the spellchecker, however, it won't necessarily catch or correct all of your grammatical errors. That's where reading out loud can help.

One last look may lead to a significant improvement in your presentation

STEP TEN

take one last look

10

The more I talk with instructors, the more they agree that wherever possible, it's smart to set your work aside for a couple of days before taking one last look at what you've created.

The reasoning is that you've been so close to your work during the writing process, that there's been no break to review what you've written with fresh eyes.

When you take that one last look, you may be sufficiently satisfied and change nothing. On the other hand, you may find that you wish to improve something you've written, provide fresh evidence to bolster an argument, or add further input that you believe would make a difference to your presentation.

This one last look is to satisfy yourself that you've done your best. It is not about perfection. I know that I can nitpick an assignment to death, changing a word here, a phrase there, without really making a difference to the overall result. So avoid "over editing."

When you know you've done your best, let the assignment stand on its own and be judged on its merits.

The following are sources to turn to for additional information, divided into **specific** and **general**:

- **Specific** deals with essay and term paper writing
- **General** refers to other sources that I believe contribute to the writing process

SPECIFIC

APA. Publication Manual of the American Psychological Association. 5th ed. Washington: American Psychological Association, 2001.

APA. APA Style. 2002. American Psychological Association. <http://www.apastyle.org>.

Baron, Alvin. Bud's Easy Research Paper Computer Manual. Lawrence: Lawrence House Publishers, 1996.

Fry, Ron. Ron Fry's How To Study Program: Write Papers. Hawthorne: Career Press, 1991.

Gibaldi, Joseph. MLA Handbook for Writers of Research Papers. 5th ed. New York: The Modern Language Association of America, 1999.

Hacker, Diana. A Writer's Reference. 4th ed. Boston: Bedford Books of St. Martin's Press, 1999.

James, Elizabeth and Carol Barkin. How to Write a Term Paper. New York: Beech Tree Books, 1991.

MLA. MLA Style. 2002. Modern Language Association. <http://www.mla.org>.

Pratt, John Clark. Writing from Scratch: The Essay. Savage: Littlefield Adams Quality Paperbacks, 1987.

GENERAL

Buzan, Tony. Head First. London: Thorsons, 2000.

Buzan, Tony. Use Your Head, revised ed. London: BBC Books, 1998.

Buzan, Tony and Barry Buzan. The Mind Map Book, revised ed. London: BBC Books, 1995.

Covey, Stephen, R. The 7 Habits of Highly Effective People. New York: Fireside/Simon & Schuster, 1990.

Goldberg, Natalie. Writing Down the Bones. Boston: Shambhala, 1986.

Klauser, Henriette Anne. Writing on Both Sides of the Brain. San Francisco: Harper, 1987.

Rico, Gabriele. Writing the Natural Way. Los Angeles: Jeremy P. Tarcher Inc., 1983.

Strunk Jr., William and E.B. White. The Elements of Style. 4th ed. Boston: Allyn & Bacon, 1999.